101 Krazy Uses for Golf Clubs

— BY OCCUPATION —

Harvey A. Levine, Author
Laura-Leigh Palmer, Illustrator

Copyright © 2021 by Harvey A. Levine.
All rights reserved. No part of this work may be reproduced or transmitted in any form or by any means, electronic or mechanical, including photocopying and recording, or by any information storage or retrieval system, without permission in writing from the author of this book.

Table of Contents

ACCOUNTANT	1	FOOD SERVER	63
AIRLINE PILOT	3	GLADIATOR	65
ARCHAEOLOGIST	5	GRAVE DIGGER	67
ARMY RECRUITER	7	HYPNOTIST	69
AUDIOLOGIST	9	INTERIOR DESIGNER	71
AUTO MECHANIC	11	JANITOR	73
BAKER	13	JOCKEY	75
BARTENDER	15	JUDGE	77
BEAUTICIAN	17	JUGGLER	79
BOUNCER	19	KNIFE THROWER	81
BURLESQUE QUEEN	21	KNITTER	83
CARDIOLOGIST	23	LANDSCAPER	85
CARPENTER	25	LIBRARIAN	87
CHEF	27	LIFE GUARD	89
CHIROPRACTOR	29	MAFIA MEMBER	91
CLOWN	31	MAGICIAN	93
COMEDIAN	33	MAID	95
CONSTRUCTION WORKER	35	MAILMAN	97
COXSWAIN	37	MARINE	99
CROUPIER	39	MATADOR	101
DANCER	41	MATCHMAKER	103
DEMOLITION WORKER	43	METEOROLOGIST	105
DENTIST	45	MINE SWEEPER	107
DETECTIVE	47	MINISTER	109
DOG TRAINER	49	MORTICIAN	111
ECONOMIST	51	MOTIVATIONAL SPEAKER	113
EPIDEMIOLOGIST	53	MOTORCYCLIST	115
EXTERMINATOR	55	MOUNTAIN CLIMBER	117
FARMER	57	NEUROSURGEON	119
FIRE FIGHTER	59	NUN	121
FLORIST	61	OB-GYN	123

OPERA SINGER	125	TOUR GUIDE	185
OPTOMETRIST	127	TRACK STAR	187
ORAL SURGEON	129	TRAVEL AGENT	189
ORCHESTRA CONDUCTOR	131	TUG BOAT OPERATOR	191
ORTHOPEDIC SURGEON	133	UBER DRIVER	193
OTOLARYNGOLOGIST	135	USHER	195
PANHANDLER	137	VIOLINIST	197
PERSONAL TRAINER	139	WINDOW WASHER	199
PIANIST	141	ZOOLOGIST	201
PIZZA MAKER	143		
PLASTIC SURGEON	145		
PLUMBER	147		
POLICEMAN	149		
POLITICIAN	151		
PRISON GUARD	153		
PROCTOLOGIST	155		
PROSTHETIC MAKER	157		
PSYCHIATRIST	159		
RABBI	161		
RAPPER	163		
ROCK STAR	165		
RUG CLEANER	167		
SEX THERAPIST	169		
SNAKE CHARMER	171		
SNIPER	173		
SUBMARINER	175		
SUMO WRESTLER	177		
TELEVISION REPAIRMAN	179		
TENNIS PLAYER	181		
TIGHTROPE PERFORMER	183		

OFF THE COURSE

Golf clubs are ubiquitous. If each of the estimated 24 million golfers in this country owned a single set of 14 clubs, around 350 million would exist. With golfers known to own many extra clubs, and even extra sets of clubs, there could be about a billion clubs "out there." The obvious purpose of these clubs is to advance a little hard ball toward a designated hole in the ground, and I have endeavored to fulfill this purpose. But like other golfers, while in the middle of a round of golf, I have used my clubs for secondary purposes.

Golf clubs are commonly referred to as "sticks," and as such, I have used them as a cane, a crutch, and a half seat to lean on while waiting to putt. On the tee box, I have used the head of a golf driver to pound a tee into the ground. Between the tee box and the green, I have used fairway woods and irons to fetch balls out of water, pull balls out of thicket, and hook balls from behind trees. Any of my irons have been used to smash loose turf back into place, to dislodge grass and dirt from my shoe cleats, and to clear leaves from in front of my ball. And finally, my golf clubs have served as potential weapons, scaring off geese, fox and an assortment of flying critters. While driving in a golf cart, I have clutched my driver while spotting alligators sunning in Florida, snakes resting along the water in Georgia, and bear moving throughout the woods in northwestern Canada. Until recently, I have not thought much about these on-course, non-playing uses of golf clubs as they were commonly practiced. But then, when the garbage disposal in my kitchen sink jammed, my thought process changed.

I needed a device to lower into the sink's disposal and force the blades to move. Not having my customary broom handy, I reached for a nearby five-iron leaning against the hallway wall. Using the end of the shaft, I quickly solved the problem. This usage got me to think about what other non-playing uses golf clubs could fulfill. I thought of the secondary applications on the course, and with such headings as: "medical devices," "tools," "weapons," and "arm extenders," I began to construct a list of potential uses, with the hope of creating an educational resource.

First on my list was the obvious — a cane. Then came a hammer, a club and a pole. But as I constructed the list, it became clear that these alternative uses were highly impractical, limited in number, not very clever, and just plain silly. If people wanted a cane — other than for a temporary emergency — they could readily purchase one for a modest price at the local drug store. I reached similar conclusions for the other items on my abbreviated list. Consequently, I put my idea to rest.

As time went on, it dawned on me that what was impractical and silly could be imaginative and humorous — especially in light of some of the more popular attitudes toward golf: that it is a game for the wealthy, that to many golfers it is more important than even family, that it's a "long walk spoiled," that it is much more mental than physical, and that to engage in it results in a love-hate relationship. To combine such perspectives with unrealistic, but possible uses of golf clubs, could result in cartoonish images with imaginative captions. What could enhance these imaginary uses would be to associate them with various occupations and in doing so, solve organizational issues. What I needed was a good illustrator. Upon the recommendation of a neighbor, I found her in Laura-Leigh Palmer. Her excellent work speaks for itself.

This is not a serious book. ENJOY it for what it is — a laugh at the game of golf, and its susceptibility to humor from the perspective of many professions.

Harvey A. Levine

ACCOUNTANT

Oh, I don't play golf. The clubs remind me that I can loosen my tie on casual Fridays.

101 Krazy Uses for Golf Clubs

National Golf Lovers Day

October 4th

AIRLINE PILOT

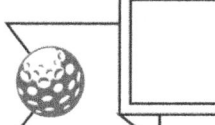

Mayday! Mayday! Request permission to land at nearest golf course. Need a tee time for two.

101 Krazy Uses for Golf Clubs

National Golf Lovers Day

October 4th

ARCHAEOLOGIST

No luck in finding relics, but I got two ancient golf balls.

101 Krazy Uses for Golf Clubs

National Golf Lovers Day

October 4th

ARMY RECRUITER

For a two-year hitch, you get the clubs.
For four years, we throw in a membership at our golf club in Afghanistan.

101 Krazy Uses for Golf Clubs

National Golf Lovers Day

October 4th

AUDIOLOGIST

Can you hear me now?

101 Krazy Uses for Golf Clubs

National Golf Lovers Day

October 4th

 # AUTO MECHANIC

That should do it. The insurance adjuster
is on his way.

101 Krazy Uses for Golf Clubs

National Golf Lovers Day

October 4th

BAKER

It's a space saver, but a pain in the butt
when a customer wants one from the bottom.

101 Krazy Uses for Golf Clubs

National Golf Lovers Day

October 4th

BARTENDER

It's our designated driver.

101 Krazy Uses for Golf Clubs

National Golf Lovers Day

October 4th

BEAUTICIAN

I'm using a strong grip, full body turn, and a follow-through. The least you can do is to keep your head still.

101 Krazy Uses for Golf Clubs

National Golf Lovers Day

October 4th

BOUNCER

Before you do anything stupid, you are warned that I'm deadly with a Mulligan.

101 Krazy Uses for Golf Clubs

National Golf Lovers Day

October 4th

BURLESQUE QUEEN

It's my "schtick."

101 Krazy Uses for Golf Clubs

National Golf Lovers Day

October 4th

CARDIOLOGIST

A round of golf is our most reliable stress test.

101 Krazy Uses for Golf Clubs

National Golf Lovers Day

October 4th

CARPENTER

It feels so good when the nail goes in the hole.

101 Krazy Uses for Golf Clubs

National Golf Lovers Day

October 4th

 # CHEF

With my low handicap, I stir fewer times.

101 Krazy Uses for Golf Clubs

National Golf Lovers Day

October 4th

CHIROPRACTOR

The 64 degree head is the perfect angle to cure your scoliosis.

101 Krazy Uses for Golf Clubs

National Golf Lovers Day

October 4th

CLOWN

This is the result of bad club selection.

101 Krazy Uses for Golf Clubs

National Golf Lovers Day

October 4th

COMEDIAN

It's my ice breaker. I bring the club out with me, take my normal swing, and people laugh.

101 Krazy Uses for Golf Clubs

National Golf Lovers Day

October 4th

CONSTRUCTION WORKER

You have to play to understand.

101 Krazy Uses for Golf Clubs

National Golf Lovers Day

October 4th

COXSWAIN

Now you know why I brought these clubs.

101 Krazy Uses for Golf Clubs

National Golf Lovers Day

October 4th

CROUPIER

Hands off the table until I finish my swing.

101 Krazy Uses for Golf Clubs

National Golf Lovers Day

October 4th

DANCER

It's a partner that always follows my lead.

41

101 Krazy Uses for Golf Clubs

National Golf Lovers Day

October 4th

DEMOLITION WORKER

She's a hacker from the local golf club.

101 Krazy Uses for Golf Clubs

National Golf Lovers Day

October 4th

DENTIST

Squeeze this club. Your insurance company doesn't pay for novacane.

101 Krazy Uses for Golf Clubs

National Golf Lovers Day

October 4th

DETECTIVE

Is this your club? Do you know
it was used to kill your ex-wife? Where were you last
Sunday when it rained?

101 Krazy Uses for Golf Clubs

National Golf Lovers Day

October 4th

DOG TRAINER

Forget your training and bury it.

101 Krazy Uses for Golf Clubs

National Golf Lovers Day

October 4th

ECONOMIST

Based on how I hit this five-iron yesterday,
I predict that the recession will end in five months,
assuming it doesn't end sooner or later.

101 Krazy Uses for Golf Clubs

National Golf Lovers Day

October 4th

EPIDEMIOLOGIST

It's a social distancing thing, but
I accept your condemnation.

101 Krazy Uses for Golf Clubs

National Golf Lovers Day

October 4th

EXTERMINATOR

As advertised, we don't use chemicals.

101 Krazy Uses for Golf Clubs

National Golf Lovers Day

October 4th

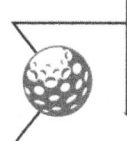

FARMER

I got the idea from the divots on the golf course.

101 Krazy Uses for Golf Clubs

National Golf Lovers Day

October 4th

FIRE FIGHTER

They don't call it a rescue club for nothing.

101 Krazy Uses for Golf Clubs

National Golf Lovers Day

October 4th

FLORIST

The golf clubs are the attraction but the profit
is in the flowers.

101 Krazy Uses for Golf Clubs

National Golf Lovers Day

October 4th

FOOD SERVER

One club sandwich coming up.

101 Krazy Uses for Golf Clubs

National Golf Lovers Day

October 4th

GLADIATOR

I suggest you lease these clubs by the hour.

101 Krazy Uses for Golf Clubs

National Golf Lovers Day

October 4th

GRAVE DIGGER

It's the request of duffers
who want to punish their clubs.

101 Krazy Uses for Golf Clubs

National Golf Lovers Day

October 4th

HYPNOTIST

You are getting sleepy. Your eyes are heavy.
You will soon be out cold.

101 Krazy Uses for Golf Clubs

National Golf Lovers Day

October 4th

INTERIOR DESIGNER

There's nothing like repurposing a failed item.

101 Krazy Uses for Golf Clubs

National Golf Lovers Day

October 4th

JANITOR

The rats hate my new sweeper.

101 Krazy Uses for Golf Clubs

National Golf Lovers Day

October 4th

JOCKEY

I only use this extended driver when the horse is a long shot.

101 Krazy Uses for Golf Clubs

National Golf Lovers Day

October 4th

JUDGE

Be Kind to Lawyers Day April 13

Order on the course. I mean, the court.
God! I hate being here on nice Wednesdays.

101 Krazy Uses for Golf Clubs

National Golf Lovers Day

October 4th

JUGGLER

It's so nice to throw clubs in the air without being penalized.

101 Krazy Uses for Golf Clubs

National Golf Lovers Day

October 4th

KNIFE THROWER

I've already lost three wives using knives,
but my girlfriend is another matter.

101 Krazy Uses for Golf Clubs

National Golf Lovers Day

October 4th

KNITTER

Knit one. Purl one. Ace. Knit two.
Purl two. Birdie. Knit three. Purl three. Par.

101 Krazy Uses for Golf Clubs

National Golf Lovers Day

October 4th

LANDSCAPER

As it says in the Bible, "Ashes to ashes. Wood to wood."

101 Krazy Uses for Golf Clubs

National Golf Lovers Day

October 4th

LIBRARIAN

Our personal-injury insurance rates have dropped since we eliminated ladders.

101 Krazy Uses for Golf Clubs

National Golf Lovers Day

October 4th

LIFE GUARD

Hold on. I need to go back and get a longer club.

101 Krazy Uses for Golf Clubs

National Golf Lovers Day

October 4th

MAFIA MEMBER

Conk him with an iron. If that doesn't
do it, take a Mulligan and use your 45.

101 Krazy Uses for Golf Clubs

National Golf Lovers Day

October 4th

MAGICIAN

Pick a club. Any club.

101 Krazy Uses for Golf Clubs

National Golf Lovers Day

October 4th

MAID

Thank goodness my golf coach fitted me
with this flexible graphite shaft.

101 Krazy Uses for Golf Clubs

National Golf Lovers Day

October 4th

MAILMAN

He's not worried. He knows
I need six swings to connect.

101 Krazy Uses for Golf Clubs

National Golf Lovers Day

October 4th

MARINE

There's nothing like this Semper Five iron.

101 Krazy Uses for Golf Clubs

National Golf Lovers Day

October 4th

MATADOR

Die! Die! Just like most of my putts.

101 Krazy Uses for Golf Clubs

National Golf Lovers Day

October 4th

MATCHMAKER

It's not a match. You are compatible in background, religion, and education, but your different club preferences is a game changer.

101 Krazy Uses for Golf Clubs

National Golf Lovers Day

October 4th

METEOROLOGIST

It looks like a 50% chance of nine holes on Sunday, dropping to 30% on Wednesday.

101 Krazy Uses for Golf Clubs

National Golf Lovers Day

October 4th

MINE SWEEPER

It's a win-win situation. Either it doesn't blow
or I finally get rid of these clubs.

101 Krazy Uses for Golf Clubs

National Golf Lovers Day

October 4th

MINISTER

Dear Lord, let it rain on Sundays,
and at least sometimes on Wednesdays.

101 Krazy Uses for Golf Clubs

National Golf Lovers Day

October 4th

MORTICIAN

The handles are an extra $500, but do you really want to deny poor Fred his last wish?

101 Krazy Uses for Golf Clubs

National Golf Lovers Day

October 4th

MOTIVATIONAL SPEAKER

It's the path not taken.

101 Krazy Uses for Golf Clubs

National Golf Lovers Day

October 4th

MOTORCYCLIST

I don't play, but if I get stopped by a cop,
he won't stereotype me as a red neck.

101 Krazy Uses for Golf Clubs

National Golf Lovers Day

October 4th

MOUNTAIN CLIMBER

It's well worth the challenge. I get an extra 20 yards in the thin air.

101 Krazy Uses for Golf Clubs

National Golf Lovers Day

October 4th

NEUROSURGEON

As I suspected, the tumor is gone.

101 Krazy Uses for Golf Clubs

National Golf Lovers Day

October 4th

NUN

The golf course is calling and I must go.

101 Krazy Uses for Golf Clubs

National Golf Lovers Day

October 4th

OB-GYN

Now I'm sure that I shouldn't have married a doctor.

101 Krazy Uses for Golf Clubs

National Golf Lovers Day

October 4th

OPERA SINGER

It's my secret to hitting a high C.

101 Krazy Uses for Golf Clubs

National Golf Lovers Day

October 4th

OPTOMETRIST

Starting from left to right, what numbered clubs can you identify?

127

101 Krazy Uses for Golf Clubs

National Golf Lovers Day

October 4th

ORAL SURGEON

I only connect about one in three times,
but I feel this is that time.

101 Krazy Uses for Golf Clubs

National Golf Lovers Day

October 4th

ORCHESTRA CONDUCTOR

It's good for slow compositions, but on up-tempo pieces the violinists are in peril.

101 Krazy Uses for Golf Clubs

National Golf Lovers Day

October 4th

ORTHOPEDIC SURGEON

This should hold until I get back from
my golf vacation.

101 Krazy Uses for Golf Clubs

National Golf Lovers Day

October 4th

OTOLARYNGOLOGIST

In the future, I suggest closing your mouth
when you make a divot.

101 Krazy Uses for Golf Clubs

National Golf Lovers Day

October 4th

PANHANDLER

If I can give up golf on a weekend, then you can certainly part with a few bucks.

101 Krazy Uses for Golf Clubs

National Golf Lovers Day

October 4th

PERSONAL TRAINER

Let's start with this junior, hollow-shaft, paper-head club, and work our way up to a senior club with a cardboard head.

101 Krazy Uses for Golf Clubs

National Golf Lovers Day

October 4th

PIANIST

Be the right club.

101 Krazy Uses for Golf Clubs

National Golf Lovers Day

October 4th

PIZZA MAKER

You want a slice? Try my five-iron.

101 Krazy Uses for Golf Clubs

National Golf Lovers Day

October 4th

PLASTIC SURGEON

This is a complicated face lift. I'll need the hybrid.

101 Krazy Uses for Golf Clubs

National Golf Lovers Day

October 4th

PLUMBER

For the good of my business, I hope this secret is not leaked to golfers.

101 Krazy Uses for Golf Clubs

National Golf Lovers Day

October 4th

POLICEMAN

These are evidence in the murders of three geese, a fox, an alligator, and two senior slow-playing hackers.

101 Krazy Uses for Golf Clubs

National Golf Lovers Day

October 4th

POLITICIAN

You scratch my back and I'll scratch yours.

101 Krazy Uses for Golf Clubs

National Golf Lovers Day

October 4th

PRISON GUARD

It's not high tech, but it works when the alarm clock breaks.

101 Krazy Uses for Golf Clubs

National Golf Lovers Day

October 4th

PROCTOLOGIST

Fore!

101 Krazy Uses for Golf Clubs

National Golf Lovers Day

October 4th

PROSTHETIC MAKER

The added advantage is that you can
carry one less club in your bag.

101 Krazy Uses for Golf Clubs

National Golf Lovers Day

October 4th

PSYCHIATRIST

When did your mother first
insist you adopt this swing?

101 Krazy Uses for Golf Clubs

National Golf Lovers Day

October 4th

RABBI

As it says in the good book, we Jews don't take a Mulligan. We take a Shapiro.

101 Krazy Uses for Golf Clubs

National Golf Lovers Day

October 4th

RAPPER

Club in a pub. Club in a pub.
Rub da club. Rub da club.
Order up.

101 Krazy Uses for Golf Clubs

National Golf Lovers Day

October 4th

ROCK STAR

Would you believe that we're self taught?

101 Krazy Uses for Golf Clubs

National Golf Lovers Day

October 4th

RUG CLEANER

With my handicap, I get 30 extra hits.

101 Krazy Uses for Golf Clubs

National Golf Lovers Day

October 4th

SEX THERAPIST

They seem to be best with threesomes.

101 Krazy Uses for Golf Clubs

National Golf Lovers Day

October 4th

SNAKE CHARMER

For some reason, my cobra loves this illegal chipper.

101 Krazy Uses for Golf Clubs

National Golf Lovers Day

October 4th

SNIPER

Not to worry. The enemy also uses clubs, and I have a lower handicap.

101 Krazy Uses for Golf Clubs

National Golf Lovers Day

October 4th

SUBMARINER

There's the slow foursome. Load torpedo one.

101 Krazy Uses for Golf Clubs

National Golf Lovers Day

October 4th

SUMO WRESTLER

Suspenders are against the rules.

101 Krazy Uses for Golf Clubs

National Golf Lovers Day

October 4th

TELEVISION REPAIRMAN

It ain't over til the new set works.

101 Krazy Uses for Golf Clubs

National Golf Lovers Day

October 4th

TENNIS PLAYER

My golf slice works wonders here.

101 Krazy Uses for Golf Clubs

National Golf Lovers Day

October 4th

TIGHTROPE PERFORMER

As Greg Norman said, "Happiness is a long walk with a putter."

101 Krazy Uses for Golf Clubs

National Golf Lovers Day

October 4th

TOUR GUIDE

Real men don't carry umbrellas.

101 Krazy Uses for Golf Clubs

National Golf Lovers Day

October 4th

TRACK STAR

It pays to have this extra-long driver.

101 Krazy Uses for Golf Clubs

National Golf Lovers Day

October 4th

TRAVEL AGENT

This should at least narrow
your choice down to a continent.

101 Krazy Uses for Golf Clubs

National Golf Lovers Day

October 4th

TUG BOAT OPERATOR

Closer! Closer! All I have is a wedge.

101 Krazy Uses for Golf Clubs

National Golf Lovers Day

October 4th

UBER DRIVER

It makes my customers realize
that I already have a back-seat driver.

101 Krazy Uses for Golf Clubs

National Golf Lovers Day

October 4th

USHER

You're in the wrong seat.

101 Krazy Uses for Golf Clubs

National Golf Lovers Day

October 4th

VIOLINIST

This bow produces different kinds of sounds, including swearing from me.

101 Krazy Uses for Golf Clubs

National Golf Lovers Day

October 4th

WINDOW WASHER

This is how I get new golf partners.
They're usually at their desks.

101 Krazy Uses for Golf Clubs

National Golf Lovers Day

October 4th

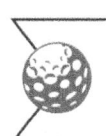

ZOOLOGIST

They're all one-irons.
Like golfers, animals also fear this club.

201

101 Krazy Uses for Golf Clubs

National Golf Lovers Day

October 4th

THE AUTHOR

HARVEY A. LEVINE

Harvey A. Levine is a retired business executive who found golf at the age of 39, when his employer offered him a membership in a golf club of his choice. As with other golfers, he developed a love/hate relationship with the game. But to this day he has relished in the humorous psychology of advancing a little ball toward a hole.

Harvey is a native of Pittsburgh, Pennsylvania. He earned a PhD in Transportation Economics and subsequently began a long career in that field eventually becoming a corporate vice president, and prior to retirement, head of his own consulting firm. He is a published author of technical books, has served as an expert witness in state and federal courts, and has consulted to both private business and government entities throughout the world. Currently residing in Potomac, Maryland, Harvey spends much of his time enjoying family, writing and painting.

101 Krazy Uses for Golf Clubs

National Golf Lovers Day

October 4th

THE ILLUSTRATOR

LAURA-LEIGH PALMER

Laura-Leigh Palmer is a graphic designer, illustrator, front-end web developer and Google Trusted Photographer with an office at Artists & Makers Studios in Rockville, Maryland. She has had a pencil in hand for almost all her life, growing up in the Western Pennsylvania and Southern West Virginia areas. She sold her first illustration at the age of four of a cat the day before it died. The owner came to her inquiring about the sketch and the artist was glad to part with it for a dollar.

She is the author of the only history of Wheaton, Maryland and she actively exhibits her fine artwork in the Washington DC area. She is available for commissions and enjoys doing murals and portraits of animals and people. She does not play golf but has done photo shoots at several charity events and finds the atmosphere very relaxing. Probably because she does not play golf.

101 Krazy Uses for Golf Clubs

National Golf Lovers Day

October 4th

THE 101 OCCUPATIONS

Accountant	Hypnotist	Panhandler
Airline Pilot	Interior Designer	Personal Trainer
Archaeologist	Janitor	Pianist
Army Recruiter	Jockey	Pizza Maker
Audiologist	Judge	Plastic Surgeon
Auto Mechanic	Juggler	Plumber
Baker	Knife Thrower	Policeman
Bartender	Knitter	Politician
Beautician	Landscaper	Prison Guard
Bouncer	Librarian	Proctologist
Burlesque Queen	Life Guard	Prosthetic Maker
Cardiologist	Mafia Member	Psychiatrist
Carpenter	Magician	Rabbi
Chef	Maid	Rapper
Chiropractor	Mailman	Rock Star
Clown	Marine	Rug Cleaner
Comedian	Matador	Sex Therapist
Construction Worker	Matchmaker	Snake Charmer
Coxswain	Meteorologist	Sniper
Croupier	Mine Sweeper	Submariner
Dancer	Minister	Sumo Wrestler
Demolition Worker	Mortician	Television Repairman
Dentist	Motivational Speaker	Tennis Player
Detective	Motorcyclist	Tightrope Walker
Dog Trainer	Mountain Climber	Tour Guide
Economist	Neurosurgeon	Track Star
Epidemiologist	Nun	Travel Agent
Exterminator	OB-GYN	Tug Boat Operator
Farmer	Opera Singer	Uber Driver
Fire Fighter	Optometrist	Usher
Florist	Oral Surgeon	Violinist
Food Server	Orchestra Conductor	Window Washer
Gladiator	Orthopedic Surgeon	Zoologist
Grave Digger	Otolaryngologist	

101 Krazy Uses for Golf Clubs

National Golf Lovers Day

October 4th

Dedicated to weekend golfers who appreciate that on the golf course 3 + 3 = 5.

THIS IS THE LAST PAGE OF THE BOOK

BUT you can maintain a relationship with the author, illustrator, and premise of this book, by inquiring about custom-made images and accompanying captions. The 101 occupations presented in the book only scratch the surface of the total number of occupations in the United States.

Harvey A. Levine and Laura-Leigh Palmer are available to customize images and captions for other occupations, and produce them both singularly and in bulk, in a professionally matted format, and protected with plastic sleeves.

For procedures and prices, Harvey A. Levine can be contacted by email (Krazygolfclubs@gmail.com), text (301-461-8766), telephone (240-386-8133), and home address (12500 Park Potomac Avenue, Apt. 206N, Potomac, MD 20854).

Made in the USA
Monee, IL
02 April 2021